KU-440-767

CONTENTS ▶

A NEW WAY TO FLY

▶ Drones give pilots an exciting way to fly. These **remote-controlled** aircraft fly in ways that few vehicles can. People all around the world enjoy flying drones. Some fly them just for fun, others compete in drone contests.

remote-controlled – controlled from a distance; remote-controlled aircraft are flown by pilots using a controller on the ground

Incredible
DRONE
COMPETITIONS

BY THOMAS K. ADAMSON

Raintree is an imprint of Capstone Global Library Limited,
a company incorporated in England and Wales having its registered office at
264 Banbury Road, Oxford, OX2 7DY – Registered company number: 6695582

www.raintree.co.uk
myorders@raintree.co.uk

Edited by Aaron Sautter
Designed by Kyle Grenz
Picture research by Eric Gohl
Production by Steve Walker
Printed and bound in China

ISBN 978 1 474 74461 4
22 21 20 19 18 17
10 9 8 7 6 5 4 3 2 1

British Library Cataloguing in Publication Data
A full catalogue record for this book is available from the British Library.

Acknowledgements
We would like to thank the following for permission to reproduce photographs:
Alamy: David Stock, 7, 8, 25, 26–27, 29; AP Photo: Nick Ut, 22; Getty Images: Anadolu Agency, 21,
Drew Angerer, 18, Sean Gallup, 17; Newscom: picture-alliance/dpa/Jan Woitas, 11; Shutterstock:
Absemetov, cover (bottom), aerogondo2, 15, Jag_cz, 5, The Polovinkin, cover (top), Tochanchai, 12

Every effort has been made to contact copyright holders of material reproduced in this book.
Any omissions will be rectified in subsequent printings if notice is given to the publisher.

All the Internet addresses (URLs) given in this book were valid at the time of going to press.
However, due to the dynamic nature of the Internet, some addresses may have changed, or sites
may have changed or ceased to exist since publication. While the author and publisher regret any
inconvenience this may cause readers, no responsibility for any such changes can be accepted by
either the author or the publisher.

0517/CA21700461 042017 4655

INCREDIBLE COMPETITIONS

▶ The world's best drone pilots compete in races, **freestyle** and combat events. Some large events give away big cash prizes to winning **contestants**.

freestyle – type of competition in which contestants free to use various tricks and moves

contestant – person who takes part in a competition

During night-time races, LED lights on drones make them easier to spot. Race courses are also often marked with neon lights.

Pilots race drones through tough courses. They don't just turn left and right. They also go over, under and through **obstacles**. Most competitions are outdoor events. Some events are held in large stadiums or empty buildings.

obstacle – object or barrier that competitors must avoid during a race

HIGH-TECH FLYING

Many pilots compete with **quadcopter** drones. Pilots often use first-person-view (FPV) goggles. These goggles allow the pilot to see what the drone "sees". It's like playing a video game in real life.

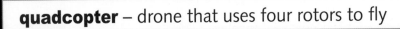

quadcopter – drone that uses four rotors to fly

camera

Most competitive drones have **high-definition** cameras. The cameras help pilots to see where drones are going during a race. Cameras also give fans a great view on TV and computer screens!

high definition – technology that displays videos or pictures with a very sharp, clear image

carbon fibre – strong, lightweight material made of very thin threads of carbon

A pilot's remote control sends radio signals to the drone. Another signal links the drone and the pilot's FPV goggles. The radio signals use different **frequencies** so that they don't get mixed up.

frequency – number of sound waves that pass a location in a certain amount of time

FACT

Remote controls for most drones have a range of about 0.8 km (0.5 miles). Some can work as far away as 6 km (3.7 miles).

DRONE BATTLES AND FREESTYLE

▶ Drone combat is like a boxing match. Pilots try to knock one another's drones out of the air. Drone combat is a test of tough drone design. Many pilots build or **modify** their drones for these events.

modify – to change or alter in some way

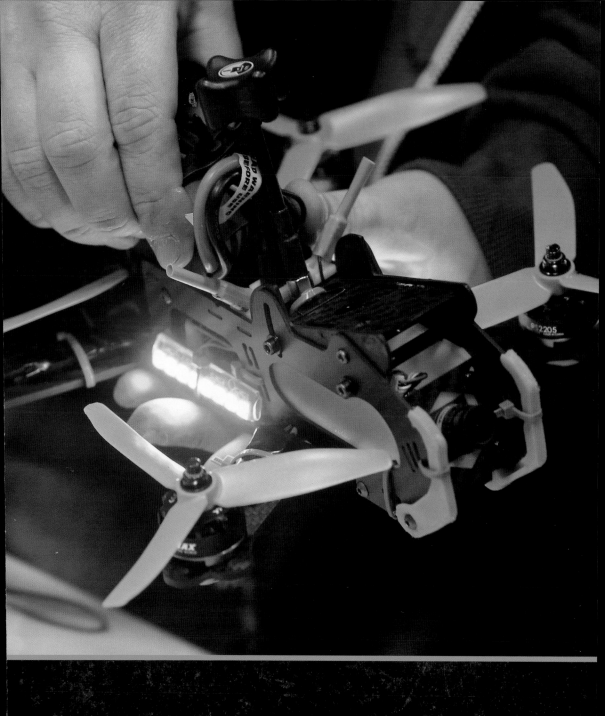

Pilots test their flying skills in freestyle competitions. Their drones do mid-air flips and spins to earn points. They may do tricks around obstacles or fly very close to water.

FACT

One freestyle trick is called the corkscrew. A drone flies in twisting circles around a bridge as it moves along the length of it.

CHAMPIONSHIP RACING

▶ In some drone races, pilots go through qualifying **heats**. Pilots with the best times move to the **elimination** rounds. The winners keep moving up until someone wins the championship.

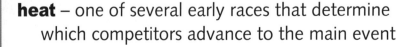

heat – one of several early races that determine which competitors advance to the main event

elimination – removed from a competition

2016 Paris Drone Festival in Paris, France

FACT

The first professional drone race in the UK was held at London's Alexandra Palace in 2017.

In the Drone Racing League, pilots earn points during the racing season. Those with the most points can compete in the World Championship race.

The first ever World Drone Prix took place in 2016. It was held in Dubai, United Arab Emirates. The pilots raced drones through brightly lit gates and other obstacles.

FACT

The World Drone Prix also included a twisting "joker lane". Pilots had to follow this special part of the course at least once during the race.

Drone Worlds took place in Hawaii in 2016. It was the world's largest drone competition. Pilots came from more than 30 countries. They competed in both racing and freestyle contests.

FACT

Pilots at Drone Worlds competed for prizes totalling $250,000.

Drone pilots compete for major awards. At the World Drone Prix, pilots were awarded prizes totalling £800,000. Skilled drone pilots will keep competing to be the best!

England's Luke Bannister (right) won the top prize at the 2016 World Drone Prix in Dubai. The 15-year-old pilot won £200,000.

Glossary

carbon fibre strong, lightweight material made of very thin threads of carbon

contestant person who takes part in a competition

elimination removed from a competition

freestyle type of competition in which competitors are free to use various tricks and moves

frequency number of sound waves that pass a location in a certain amount of time

heat one of several early races that determine which competitors advance to the main event

high definition technology that displays videos or pictures with a very sharp, clear image

modify to change or alter in some way

obstacle object or barrier that competitors must avoid during a race

quadcopter drone that uses four rotors to fly

remote-controlled controlled from a distance; remote-controlled aircraft are flown by pilots using a controller on the ground

Read more

Audacious Aviators (Ultimate Adventurers),
Jen Green (Raintree, 2015)

Computers (Jobs if You Like), Charlotte Guillain
(Raintree, 2013)

Recreational Drones (Drones), Matt Chandler
(Raintree, 2017)

Websites

www.bbc.co.uk/newsround/32691021
What are rules for flying drones? Find out more!

www.bbc.co.uk/newsround/32142774
See what drones can do! Watch this video of a drone
herding sheep.

Index